FRANCIS XAVIER
and the Samurai's Lost Treasure

Written by
Fernando Uribe and Dan Engler

Art Design
Egidio Dal Chele

Art Painting
Craig Gardner
Richard Martin

© MCMXCIII Creative Communication Center, N.V.
De Ruyterkade 62
Curaçao, Netherlands Antilles

Back in 1529, at school in Paris, young Francis Xavier had fun being the smartest student and the best at sports.

His roommate and best friend, Ignatius of Loyola, cheered for him: "Bravo, Francis. You won the big race again!"

After the race, as Francis was leaving for a party...

"Francis, wait!" yelled a student with a message from Francis's parents in Spain.

But Francis was gone. So the student told Ignatius instead: "They can't send Francis any more money to keep him in school!"

Ignatius wanted to help Francis before having to tell him the bad news. So he secretly worked hard every night...

...and left Francis all the money he made.

Francis thought his parents were sending the pouches, but wondered why they were different and had less money than before.

Thinking Ignatius might be stealing some of the money, Francis followed him, and found out what Ignatius was really doing!

Back in their room, Francis told Ignatius,
"I'm sorry for thinking you were bad!"

Ignatius said, "Never mind. I'm glad to
help! Jesus wants us to give, not take."

"Ignatius, help me follow Jesus as you do!" asked Francis.

And so, later on, they became priests. Ignatius named their new group the Company of Jesus, today known as Jesuits.

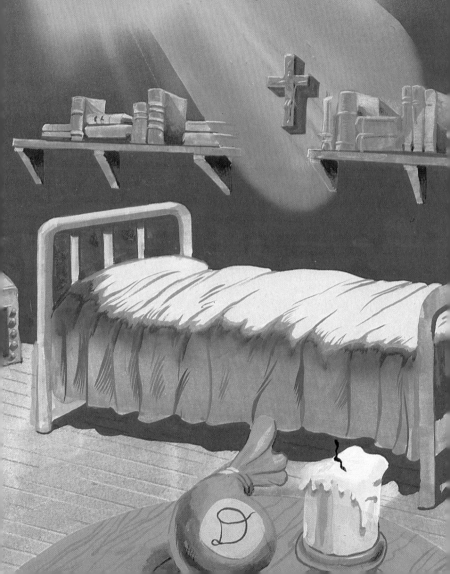

Their goal was to help the Pope bring everybody closer to Jesus. Francis was happy when told to do that in far-off India.

In India, as Francis looked at his map for the way to a village of pearl divers...

"Look, Shish. He's lost!" said a boy named Kammu to his pet monkey.

Francis and Kammu saved each other from a tiger. From that moment on, they became very good friends.

In the village, Kammu's mom Sunita and dad Kumar were sad: "Pirates came and stole the pearls we need to pay the taxes!"

Mean tax collector Ratji and greedy Malo said, "If you don't get more pearls for us real fast, we'll take everything you own!"

Later, Francis told Kumar, "Let's ask God for strength to fix up the village and find enough pearls in time."

The people were happy when Francis told
them about Jesus. Soon they were baptized.
With hard work and Francis's help, they
fixed up the village and found lots of pearls.

Only one person was still sad: Yajiro, a samurai, or soldier, from far-off Japan.

Francis wanted Yajiro to be baptized too. But Yajiro said, "I'm too busy trying to find a black pearl for the Emperor in Japan."

Yajiro explained, "A few years back, a bad man stole the Emperor's black pearl and said I took it. I must prove I'm honest!"

Francis asked God to help Yajiro find his treasure. Once, Francis's crucifix fell into the sea and landed on a big oyster. Yajiro quickly got the crucifix — and the oyster.

Yajiro gave the oyster to Kammu. As
Yajiro left, Kammu opened the oyster and...
"Samurai, come back! You found your black
pearl!" Kammu yelled.

Yajiro was happy, but then he heard Malo and Ratji planning to steal the pearls and have the pirates wreck the village — again!

When the pirates attacked, Francis stood up to them with only his crucifix. The pirate chief was impressed: "I admire your courage and faith, so we'll leave you alone!"

Then, as Malo and Ratji were trying to
sneak away with the chest of pearls...

"These aren't pearls, they're bees! OWW!"
cried Malo. "OUCH!" Ratji hollered as they
ran away. They didn't know Kammu and
Yajiro had replaced the pearls with bees.

Later, Francis and Yajiro went to Japan. Francis wanted the Emperor to let him tell people about Jesus. Yajiro wanted to give the new black pearl to the Emperor.

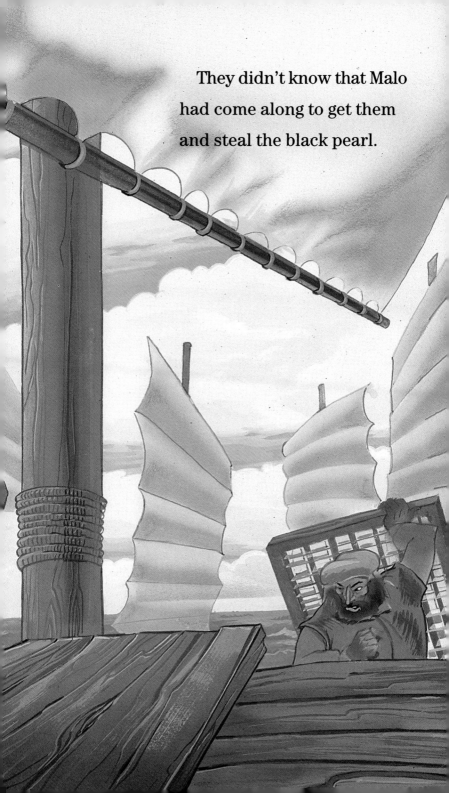

They didn't know that Malo
had come along to get them
and steal the black pearl.

Yajiro left to get some fancy clothes so he would look important for the Emperor. But Francis went to the palace in his simple clothes. The guards said, "Leave, beggar!"

As Francis left, he heard the voice of...
Malo! He was telling a bad samurai named
Nomo, "We must stop Francis, and get Yajiro
and his black pearl."

Disguised as rich visitors, Yajiro and Francis finally got inside the palace. But Francis lost his wig. Now Malo and Nomo knew who they were!

Malo told Yajiro, "I'll hurt Francis unless you give us the pearl." Nomo got the pearl, but it fell and rolled into a crocodile pond! Nomo was going to attack Yajiro, when...

"Wait!" said Francis to Nomo. "I'll get the pearl if you let Yajiro go."

Trusting in God, Francis jumped in, got the pearl, and came out — unhurt!

Just then, the Emperor showed up — he had seen everything! He told Malo and Nomo, "So *you* stole my old black pearl! Now I'll throw you to the crocodiles!"

But Francis got the Emperor to change his mind. The Emperor liked Francis and said, "I will let you tell my people about Jesus."

The Emperor told Yajiro to keep the pearl.
"Thank you, Majesty," said Yajiro, "but it is
for you. I have found another treasure of
much greater beauty and value..."

"...It is Francis Xavier's God on the Cross. He is the Master I now wish to serve."

Francis was happy. Yajiro had found the real Treasure at last.